G000242256

conceptions

POPULAR MYTHS DEBUNKED AND DISPELLED
FROM THE PAGES OF FORTEAN TIMES

WRITTEN BY
Mat Coward

ILLUSTRATED BY
Hunt Emerson

EDITED BY
David Sutton

DESIGN
Etienne Gilfillan

www.forteantimes.com

PUBLISHING & MARKETING
Paul Rayner
020 7907 6663
paul_rayner@dennis.co.uk

MAGBOOK PUBLISHER
Dharmesh Mistry
020 7907 6100
dharmesh_mistry@dennis.co.uk

MAGBOOK

The MagBook brand is a trademark of Dennis
Publishing Ltd, 30 Cleveland St, London W1T 4JD.
Company registered in England. All material
© Dennis Publishing Ltd, licensed by Felden 2013,
and may not be reproduced in whole or part
without the consent of the publishers.
Mythconceptions ISBN 1-78106-148-3

LICENSING & SYNDICATION
To license this product please contact Carlotta
Serantoni on +44 (0) 20 79076550 or email
carlotta_serantoni@dennis.co.uk
To syndicate content from this product please
contact Anj Dosaj Halai on +44(0) 20 7907 6132
or email anj_dosaj-halai@dennis. co.uk

DIGITAL PRODUCTION MANAGER:
Nicky Baker

MANAGEMENT
MagBook Publisher: Dharmesh Mistry
Operations Director: Robin Ryan
MD of Advertising: Julian Lloyd-Evans
Newstrade Director: David Barker
MD of Enterprise: Martin Belson
Chief Operating Officer: Brett Reynolds
Group Finance Director: Ian Leggett
Chief Executive: James Tye
Chairman: Felix Dennis

Produced for Dennis Publishing by Wild Talents Ltd
Printed at Polestar Stones

introduction

I started sometime in the 1980s, with two Well Known Facts: Hitler was a vegetarian, and Sweden had the world's highest suicide rate. These were things which everyone, including me, had grown up knowing, and which I had discovered, by chance, were not true. I wondered if there were any more ...

By 1998, I had managed to accumulate perhaps a dozen such stories – enough to offer them to the editors of **Fortean Times** as a short series. Fifteen years later, the column is still running. It sometimes seems there is no end to the number of things which everyone knows to be true, but which aren't.

Or *might* not be. A crucial element of the Mythconceptions format is the "Disclaimer." It would be against the spirit of **Fortean Times** to ever claim that anything it publishes represents something as un-fortean as the final truth. Unfortunately, not all readers notice the disclaimer; I do get angry letters from people, upset at my errors, or perhaps simply that I've tickled their sacred cows. I always tell them the same thing: don't write to me, write to the magazine's letters page! More than anything else, the purpose of the Mythconceptions column is to stimulate debate.

In the magazine, these columns often end with a request for further information on a matter which I, or a reader, suspect might turn out to be Mythconception material. I hope that readers of this magbook will also feel free to send in ideas for new Mythconceptions, or requests for answers to that popular question: "Can that *really* be true?" **Post them to Fortean Times, PO Box 2409, London NW5 4NP or email to sieveking@forteantimes.com.**

For me, the greatest pleasure of writing this column over the years has been the opportunity to collaborate with Hunt Emerson, one of this country's finest cartoonists. I hope you'll enjoy the myths and debunkings collected here – I *know* you'll enjoy the pictures.

Mat Coward, Summer 2013

mythconceptions

CONTENTS

1. The cat's whiskers and other animal tales

Do ostriches bury their heads in the sand?
Can a hornet sting kill you?
Did Jimi Hendrix's parrots colonise London?

CATS' WHISKERS

THE MYTH

Cats use their whiskers to balance. If, for any reason, they suffer damaged whiskers, they are no longer able to balance.

THE "TRUTH"

The idea that a cat employs its splendid whiskers in much the same way as a Victorian tightrope walker would his long bendy pole is surprisingly widely held. It's hard to imagine where it might have originated; in fact, balance in cats, as in humans, is largely a function of the inner ear. Cats have what is called "tactile hair" on various parts of their bodies, most noticeably growing out of their faces. Their whiskers, or vibrissae, are deeply rooted, heavily endowed with nerve endings, and very mobile, and provide detailed information concerning air currents and air pressure. They are mainly used for navigation in low light, and for helping to determine the direction from which prey odours and movements are coming.

DISCLAIMER

It seems that whiskers are still slightly mysterious - for instance, authorities disagree on whether or not a cat uses them to judge the width of its body, thus avoiding entering spaces which are too tight for it.

SOURCES

RSPCA Complete Cat Care Manual, Dr Andrew Edney (Dorling Kindersley, 2006)
Cat Owner's Home Veterinary Handbook (third edition), Debra Eldredge et al (Wiley Publishing, 2008)
http://s.coop/cathealth; http://s.coop/rspca

THE DEADLY HORNET

THE MYTH

Wasp and bee stings hurt, but hornet stings kill: "Seven stings to kill a horse, three a man and two a child." Throughout Europe, the hornet is feared for its ferocity and for the awesome power of its poison.

THE "TRUTH"

Hornets are the largest of the European wasps, and that's probably where their problems began: they are big, noisy and frightening. They are not, however, aggressive, and are unlikely to sting unless under attack. Even if you are stung, you won't die or become ill (except in rare cases of allergy, of course, as with all stinging insects). Analysis of hornet poison suggests that a grown man would need to be stung about 1,000 times to receive a fatal dose – and since a successful colony contains around 400 individuals, your chances of suffering such a fate might be considered slim. Bee stings, evolved for use against honey-raiding vertebrates, are considerably stronger than those of wasps and hornets, which are used against insect prey. However, because hornet poison contains five per cent acetylcholine, the sting may be slightly more painful than those of other wasps or bees. Incidentally, some wasp stings can cause infection – but hornet stings are clean, as they don't feed carrion to their young.

DISCLAIMER

I admit it – I haven't put this one to the test; mainly because I don't have a horse handy. Some books and websites still stick to the demon stingers line, though without supporting evidence; if you can help debunk or reinstate this legend, please give *Fortean Times* a buzz.

SOURCES

www.muenster.org/hornissenschutz/hornets.htm
www.bbc.co.uk/nature/life/Europeanhornet
www.lost-in-france.com/wildlife-in-france/301-frelon-european-hornet

OSTRICHES

THE MYTH

Ostriches, when frightened, bury their heads in the sand. By analogy, anyone who refuses to face an uncomfortable truth is said to be behaving like an ostrich.

THE "TRUTH"

Good news for the theory of natural selection: the ostrich does not react to danger by hiding its bonce. Ostriches have powerful legs, with pickaxe-type claws. An ostrich kick is sufficient to open a man's stomach; such human fatalities are not unknown. They are the world's largest birds, and can react aggressively if attacked. Alternatively, they can flee, as, though flightless, they are capable of achieving considerable land speeds. When feeding, an ostrich will often lay its head flat on the ground; from a distance, the long, thin neck might seem to end at sand-level. This, perhaps, is the origin of the misunderstanding; though, if so, we have to assume that the founders of this popular myth never actually got very close to any ostriches. Which is understandable: ostriches are big and fierce.

DISCLAIMER

Or are we just running away from the facts here? If you want to stand up for the subterranean noggin position, don't be shy – write in.

SOURCES

www.abc.net.au/science/articles/2006/11/02/1777947.htm
http://science.howstuffworks.com/zoology/birds/ostrich-meat.htm

CHAMELEONS

THE MYTH

Chameleons change colour to camouflage themselves.

THE "TRUTH"

They don't (except coincidentally). The idea that chameleons match themselves to the background as a way of becoming invisible – undoubtedly the best-known "fact" about them – is an ancient one, but its debunking also occurred BC. They do indeed change colour – but the main purpose of doing so is rather the opposite of what's assumed. They do it, not to hide, but to communicate. Males change colour to contest dominance with other males and to attract females, while females do it to display their receptiveness to mating. Mood change also alters skin colour; some species turn dark when angry, to signal their readiness to rumble. Finally, colour change can help a chameleon to reflect excessive sunlight, or to absorb more heat. Some other animals, incidentally, *do* actually change colour for camouflage reasons – but not chameleons.

DISCLAIMER

Sometimes the truth itself is not easy to spot; feel free to disagree with any or all the above on *FT*'s letters page.

SOURCES

www.pulseplanet.com/archive/Sep05/3537.html
www.wildwatch.com/resources/other/chameleon.asp

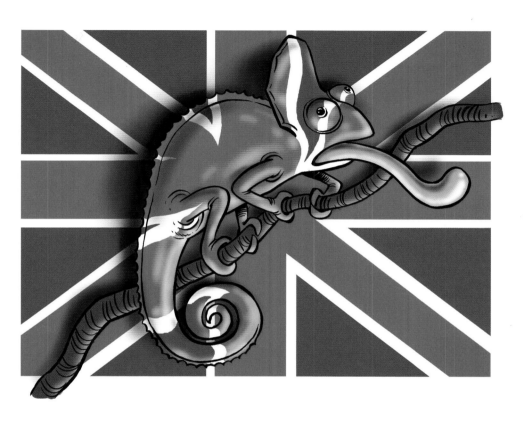

CAT YEARS

THE MYTH

One year in the life of a cat (or dog, or sometimes horse) is equivalent, in terms of lifespan, to seven human years.

THE "TRUTH"

So, if your ginger tom is 12 years old, that means he is at the same level of senescence as an 84-year-old human. In which case, how come he can still leap from the floor to the kitchen counter without apparent effort? Can your granddad do that – with or without his teeth in? Any Well Known Fact which contains the number seven tends to set the Myth-sense tingling, and the idea that the ageing process can be compared so precisely across species, despite numerous variables, is rejected by all authorities. A widely accepted approximate formula for comparing cats with humans suggests that kittens mature much faster than babies, with the rate of feline ageing slowing down significantly after two years. Therefore, for instance, a one-year-old cat might be roughly 16 in human years, while a four-year-old could be compared to a man of 32.

DISCLAIMER

Expert opinion varies considerably on this matter; there is no universally agreed feline-to-human ageing ratio.

SOURCES

In Praise of Older Cats, Sarah Hartwell (Cats Protection League, 1996)

You and Your Cat , David Taylor (Dorling Kindersley, 1986)

www.catsplay.com/thedailycat/2002-06-03/bringinghealthy/humanyears/humanyears.html

HYENAS

Hyenas are scavengers, not hunters.

Everyone who's ever watched TV knows how hyenas feed: they wait until the big cats have finished their meals, and then skulk in to mop up the leftovers. In fact, this myth was largely overthrown in the 1970s, when researchers first began to study spotted hyenas (one of four species of *Hyaenidae*) in detail. Spotties hunt mostly alone, taking, for instance, zebras, wildebeest and kudu. They can eat a third of their own body weight at one tuck-in, consuming entire animals, bones included. Hyenas and lions are direct competitors for prey, and commonly steal each other's kills – hence the classic picture of the sulky hyena awaiting the crumbs from the lion's table. But sometimes, it's the hyenas who drive off the lions. Hyenas and lions have been observed fighting in large numbers, over territory as well as food; further evidence that their relative positions in the food chain are not far apart. Hyenas (which are unrelated to dogs, incidentally) will scavenge when fresh prey is unavailable, but they are no more scavengers than lions are. In some areas, lions have been recorded stealing more from hyenas than vice versa. Some zoologists say hyenas are better hunters than lions – they can run fast and for a long time – but they do have one weakness. At a kill they emit their legendary "giggling," which brings lions and other thieves running for their share.

Hyenas remain understudied and myth-shrouded – so feel free to rip the guts out of this story, laughing maniacally the while, over on the letters page.

SOURCES

Western Daily Press, 16 Dec 2006

www.napleszoo.com/New/hyena%20release.htm

THE PARAKEETS OF LONDON

THE MYTH

The colonies of wild parakeets in London and south-east England are descended from birds which Jimi Hendrix released in the 1960s to add some psychedelic colour to the city. Either that, or the original breeding pair were Jimi's pets, accidentally released after the guitarist's death. Or, if not, then they were escapees from Shepperton film studios during the filming of *The African Queen* (1950); or possibly, in the 1970s, during the making of another film. One way or another, the London parakeets had showbiz origins.

THE "TRUTH"

Feral parrots have been recorded in London since 1855. A study by Oxford University biologists of the rose-ringed, or ring-necked, parakeet (*Psitacula krameri*) suggests that London's large parrot population has grown from fewer than 500 in 1983. They are long-lived birds with no natural predators in Britain, and it's feared they could become serious pests to agriculture and biodiversity. They are now found as far west as Wales and as far north as Glasgow. There are already more parakeets in London than there are nightingales. Their recent population explosion is perhaps explained by a warmer climate, and by the spread of garden bird-feeders. The likeliest explanation for their origins, say experts, is disappointingly mundane: they probably escaped, and were released, from aviaries, pet shops and private homes. Quick – close that window!

DISCLAIMER

There seems to be no evidence for any celebrity involvement in the parrotisation of London – but if you know better then please squawk the truth from the rooftops.

SOURCES

http://news.nationalgeographic.co.uk/news/2004/07/0708040708feralparrots.htm
http://news.bbc.co.uk/local/surrey/hi/peopleandplaces/nature/newsid8286000/8286707.stm

EVOLVING HEDGEHOGS

THE MYTH

Because the number one killer of hedgehogs today is the motor car, the animal is evolving out of its old habit of rolling up into a spiny ball in the face of danger. Natural selection is killing off the "roll up" gene, and favouring the "Run like hell" gene.

THE "TRUTH"

No one seems to know where this superficially sensible-sounding, but completely unsupported, hypothesis began. The world's number one expert on the European hedgehog, Pat Morris, writes of having first heard it in the mid-1970s, and says that it was given a boost in 1995, when it was used in a GCSE exam paper. We can safely call it a Mythconception simply because there isn't a shred of evidence to suggest it's true – but more than that, Morris and others have pointed out that it's based on a fallacy. A stationery hog is only in danger from a car if it's in line with the wheels; an animal running across the path of the vehicle is more likely to come into line with the wheels, while one running in a straight line is in no more or less danger than it would be if it stayed still. So rolling up is, mathematically, a better strategy than running.

DISCLAIMER

There's no evidence for it, and its reasoning is flawed – but of course that doesn't necessarily mean it's not happening. If you have proof either way, please roll it up and send it to the letters page.

SOURCES

The New Hedgehog Book, Pat Morris (Whittet Books, 2006)
A Prickly Affair, Hugh Warwick (Allen Lane, 2008)

2. Drowning in the Dead Sea and other deadly delusions

Are we running out of brain cells?

Did Mama Cass choke to death on a sandwich?

Did the Wall Street Crash see financiers jumping out of windows?

WALL STREET JUMPERS

THE MYTH

The Wall Street Crash of October 1929 led to dozens of ruined financiers leaping to their deaths from New York skyscrapers.

THE "TRUTH"

Without doubt, stockbrokers hurling themselves from high windows is still the defining image of the Crash; it's the one "fact" most of us know about 1929. Yet, JK Galbraith's 1955 book about the Crash systematically debunked the general belief that the failure of the stock market led to an immediate leap in the suicide rate for New York. Using official figures, he showed that the number of suicides for that period was merely average. Although there were reports of two individuals in Wall Street in 1929 ending their worries by hurling themselves from the nth floor, most suicides stuck to the traditional means, such as ropes, revolvers or rivers. The "mass leaping" myth seems to have originated in the British popular press – which perhaps could not resist a little gloat at the misfortunes of a rival empire. Interestingly, although the US press at the time refuted the story, it was subsequently as widely believed in the USA as elsewhere.

DISCLAIMER

Galbraith stated categorically of the supposed post-Crash "suicide wave" that "In fact, there was none." If you have contrary evidence, please jump in.

SOURCES

Daily Mail, 30 November 2002
Relevant extracts from John Kenneth Galbraith's *The Great Crash: 1929* can be found on the internet

THE QUICK OUTNUMBER THE DEAD

THE MYTH

There are more people alive on Earth today than have ever died. In some versions, 75 per cent of all humans who've ever lived are alive right now.

THE "TRUTH"

No one's entirely sure when this belief first became common currency (unless *you* can tell us, of course), but it appears to have become an uncritically accepted fact sometime in the 1970s. It's especially popular with those who believe overpopulation to be the world's greatest problem, with US creationists and with right-wing opponents of the welfare state. Obviously, it can never be answered definitively, because we don't know precisely how long humans have existed, or how many of them have existed. But there does seem to be a consensus amongst secular demographers that the global population in 40,000 BC was about 500,000, and reached 1 billion by AD 1800. That would mean (according to widely accepted methods of working out average death rates) that the number of deaths during those centuries alone would be around 60 billion; the current global population is around 7 billion. If these estimates are even *vaguely* right, then not only do we not yet outnumber the dead, but it's unlikely that we ever will.

DISCLAIMER

We never claim to Know The Truth – and especially not when there's statistics involved. The two sides of this debate should feel free to battle it out on *FT*'s letters page, until none are left standing.

SOURCES

www.scientificamerican.com/article.cfm?id=fact-or-fiction-living-outnumber-dead
www.bbc.co.uk/news/magazine-16870579

THE LAST VICTIM

THE MYTH

The last soldier killed in action in World War One, as everyone knows, was George Lawrence Price, a Canadian, who was shot by a German sniper just two minutes before the ceasefire.

THE "TRUTH"

The Armistice was signed at around 5am on 11 November 1918, but it was agreed that the actual war wouldn't end until 11am. This delay gave plenty more young men the chance to lose their lives in the service of imperialism and the arms trade. One man known to have beaten Price's grim record was US private Henry Gunther, machine-gunned at 10.59am in Chaumont-devant-Damvillers – but there may well have been others. One historian has calculated that that last day produced 11,000 casualties – more than on D-Day in 1944. This figure includes hundreds of fatalities; in those final hours of the war, many generals continued to sacrifice their men in full-scale military operations. One US general insisted on capturing a French town, at the cost of 300 American casualties, so that his surviving men could use the public baths.

DISCLAIMER

Can the identity of the last man to die ever truly be known? What about the many killed *after* the ceasefire? Or those who died after 11am, from wounds received before?

SOURCES

http://news.bbc.co.uk/1/hi/magazine/7696021.stm

BOILED FROGS

THE MYTH

If you place a frog in a pot of boiling water it will, unsurprisingly, attempt to escape. However, if you put the frog in tepid water, and steadily increase the temperature, it will allow itself to be boiled. This is because frogs have evolved to react to sudden changes in their environment, not to incremental ones.

THE "TRUTH"

This story has been popular since at least the mid-1990s, especially in the USA. It's employed as a parable by people as diverse as environmentalists and pro-gun campaigners, often to warn that "They" plan to take our rights away from us through a cunning programme of stealthy gradualism. By the time we realise we've been unmanned by Them, it'll be too late. Wake up and smell the amphibians! It's also extremely popular amongst "management consultants," whatever they are. Biologists and other scientists, on the other hand, dismiss it as straightforward nonsense. When the water gets too hot the frog will, of course, try to escape. Not only that, but a frog put into boiling water would *not* jump out – because it would be physically incapable of doing so.

DISCLAIMER

I'd love to know exactly where and when this story first arose – and, indeed, why. I'm assuming it's untrue, though if you wish to leap to its defence, please do so... but I'd prefer not to hear from weirdoes who've actually conducted frog-boiling experiments, ta very much.

SOURCES

www.fastcompany.com/online/01/frog.html
www.conservationmagazine.org/2011/03/frog-fable-brought-to-boil/

MAMA CASS

American rock star Mama "Cass" Elliot died from choking on a ham sandwich.

THE "TRUTH"

Her career had been faltering for some time when, in 1974, Elliot was booked to play the London Palladium. But on 29 July, she died in her hotel room. A week later, an autopsy found the cause of death to be a heart attack, with no traces of food found in her trachea; but by then the legend was firmly established – the extremely overweight singer had choked to death on a sandwich. Initial reports, given to journalists by the first doctor on the scene, supposedly provided the basis for the myth. The charming detail that it was a *ham* sandwich seems to have been added later, for obvious symbolic reasons: a fat pig had died eating a pig. (An uneaten sandwich was apparently found on her nightstand; its flavour is not, as far as I can discover, known to history.)

DISCLAIMER

There doesn't seem to be much doubt about this one – but since doubt is our precious currency, I would be pleased to hear from any reader able to supply some.

SOURCES

www.casselliot.com/biography.htm
www.imdb.com/name/nm0254177/bio

THE FIRST RAILWAY FATALITY

THE MYTH

19th century statesman William Huskisson was the first person killed by a train.

THE "TRUTH"

He may have been the first *famous* railway victim, but he was not the first. William Huskisson, Member of Parliament for Liverpool, fell into the path of Stephenson's Rocket at Parkside on 15 September 1830, during celebrations to mark the opening of the Liverpool and Manchester Railway, and died hours later of his injuries. The L&MR was the world's first full railway service, and Huskisson's lasting fame was quickly cemented. *The Times,* in its obituary of Lord Palmerston (18 October 1865), referred to "Poor Huskisson," who was "all his life a bungler. He was always in difficulties through his clumsiness, which was physical as well as moral. He was always stumbling over chairs, tripping against ropes as he landed from steamboats, breaking his shins upon stones, until at last he was knocked down and killed outright by the first railway train." But in fact, the parish register of Egglescliffe, near Stockton-on-Tees, records the death in 1827 (1825 in some sources) of an unknown female, possibly a "blind beggar woman," who was "killed by the steam machinery on the railway."

DISCLAIMER

Presumably, there must have been even earlier deaths – of navvies, for instance – in the pre-history of railways, but there, perhaps, it depends how you define your terms. If you have details to add which might get us onto the right lines, please feel free to let off steam on the *FT* letters page.

SOURCES

The Milk Jug was a Goat, Chris Birch (Pegasus, 2008)
Great Victorian Lives (Times Books, 2007)
www.btp.police.uk/aboutus/ourhistory/detailedhistory.aspx
www.egglescliffeandeaglescliffe-pc.org.uk/history.php

BRAIN CELLS

THE MYTH

You can't grow more brain cells. Every human starts with a finite number, some of which are destroyed – and never replaced – every time we figure out what two plus two makes, or try to remember where we've left our glasses.

THE "TRUTH"

This still prevalent belief was expelled from the halls of orthodoxy some years ago, when scientists discovered that all vertebrate animals continue to produce new neurons (brain cells) throughout their lives, in at least some parts of the brain. More recently, it has been shown that the fresh cells are actively involved in the formation of memory. Other studies strongly suggest that some types of anti-depressants work by causing new neuron growth – and that depression itself can inhibit brain cell replacement. Readers will be unsurprised to learn that evidence for adult neuron growth was first presented in the 1960s, and again in the 1980s, but was dismissed out of hand for no reason other than that it contradicted existing (untestable) theories.

DISCLAIMER

Most of the evidence so far seems to pertain to that shamefully persecuted species, the laboratory rat; historically-minded readers might remember that it was pioneering vivisection work which proved beyond doubt that heroin was utterly non-addictive.

SOURCES

www.mult-sclerosis.org/news/Mar2001/TheBrainMakesNewNeurons.html
http://mentalhealth.about.com/cs/psychopharmacology/a/neurogenesis.htm
www.newscientist.com/channel/being-human/brain/mg16522254.200
New York Times, 30 Oct 1998.

DROWNING IN THE DEAD SEA

THE MYTH

You can't drown in the Dead Sea – the high concentration of salt in the water produces such buoyancy that it is impossible for a human body to sink.

THE "TRUTH"

In 2010, 21 swimmers on the Israeli side of the Dead Sea had to be saved from drowning by lifeguards, and a quarter of all "recent" drownings in Israeli waters have been in the Dead Sea, according to the MDA, Israel's national disaster and rescue service. Instead of swimming below the surface with your head above it, as in a normal ocean, in the Dead Sea – which is 10 times saltier – most of you is floating on top of the water. This does, indeed, more or less rule out *sinking*. But it's precisely that which makes the place so deadly. In normal waters, if a swimmer gets his face in the water he can right himself by pushing down with his legs, or use his arms to roll over. In the buoyancy of the Dead Sea, this is extremely difficult. Experienced bathers take care to stay on their backs; those who, through misadventure or misjudgement, turn onto their fronts are the ones who get into distress.

DISCLAIMER

I remind readers that this column never claims final correctness on any matter; disputations via the letters page are positively encouraged.

SOURCES

www.jpost.com/Israel/Article.aspx?id=185232
www.ynetnews.com/articles/0,7340,L-3874630,00.html
www.mdais.com/316/5006.htm; http://io9.com/5798844/why-so-many-people-drown-in-the-dead-sea

3. Catherine the Great's horse and other sexual fallacies

Are bald men more virile?
Are rhino horns used as aphrodisiacs?
Can a medical test tell if a woman is a virgin?

VICTORIA AND THE LESBIANS

THE MYTH

Lesbianism was never made illegal in Britain because when Queen Victoria was shown the proposed legislation she refused to sign it, as she wouldn't believe that lesbians existed: "Women do not do such things." In other versions of the story, government ministers struck out all references to women in the Act, because they couldn't think of a way of explaining matters to the dear old queen.

THE "TRUTH"

The idea that Victoria refused to sign the Labouchere Amendment to the Criminal Law Amendment Act 1885, until it had been de-lesbianised, is easily dealt with: the British monarch in the late 19th century did not have the power to overrule parliament – any attempt to do so would have triggered a political earthquake. The myth apparently started in Wellington, New Zealand, in 1977, to explain why a demonstration for lesbian equality centred on a statue of Vicky. Labouchere's true motives for criminalising male homosexuality are still disputed; what seems certain is that banning *female* homosexuality never crossed his mind. Some historians suggest that the male establishment avoided legislating on lesbianism for fear of drawing women's attention to its existence.

DISCLAIMER

This must be one of the most widely-accepted and repeated beliefs this column has ever covered; if you can come up with a contemporary source to support it, then please get your sensible shoes over to the letters column and tell all.

SOURCES

Inventing the Victorians, Matthew Sweet (Faber, 2001)
www.mikedash.com/extras/forteana/ask-bizarre/victoria

THE CHASTITY BELT

THE MYTH

When mediaeval knights went gallivanting off around the world teaching foreigners not to be so uppity, they locked up their wives' naughty-but-nice-bits in contraptions made of leather and iron, to protect their bloodlines from extramarital contamination. Other than by master locksmiths, I suppose.

THE "TRUTH"

Titter ye not! Modern scholars argue that the chastity belt never existed – except, perhaps, when worn by prisoners for their own protection. In 1996, the British Museum declared to be fake a belt which it had been exhibiting since 1846. Other museums quietly removed belts from display, or even redesignated them as olde worlde dogge collars. Sotheby's said that it no longer believed there were any "genuinely used" belts in existence – news which will surprise many fetishists. Historians suggest that the chastity belt was dreamt up by French satirists such as Rabelais, and that the myth was revived by the (kinky or puritanical – take your pick) Victorians.

DISCLAIMER

The idea that chastity belts have always been what they are today – jokey curiosities – is a tempting one. But we are too cautious to accept that contemporary historians are automatically more accurate than those of former ages. If you can help to unlock this mystery, we yearn for your input.

SOURCES

"Damsels not distressed by medieval chastity belt," *Sunday Times*, 23 June 1996
www.medievalists.net/2009/01/18/the-myth-of-the-medieval-chastity-belt/

DROIT DU SEIGNEUR

THE MYTH

**"The right of the lord"(or *jus primae noctis*, "law of the first night")
refers to a legal perk enjoyed by every feudal guv'nor in mediaeval
Europe – that of bedding the brides of his vassals on their wedding
nights.**

THE "TRUTH"

The film *Braveheart* - laughingly referred to as an historical epic in Hollywood –
introduced this myth to a new generation, but some of us remember being taught
it at school. For many generations it was a generally accepted historical fact; at
least at the lower levels of academia. Today, the idea is entirely discredited; no
contemporary reference to such a practice has ever been found by historians
(although the *Encyclopedia Britannica* rather snootily suggests that it may have
existed in primitive – i.e., non-European – societies). If it happened at all, it must
have been both local and short-lived. The germ of the story is probably an 18th
century misunderstanding (or romanticisation) of the various taxes and fees
which a vassal had to pay his lord to obtain permission to marry.

DISCLAIMER

This one seems to have been thoroughly put to bed – but if you know better,
you'd better let us know.

SOURCES

www.jstor.org/discover/10.2307/3812958?uid=3738032&uid=2129&uid=2&uid=70&uid=4&sid=21102009854361
www.fibri.de/jus/arthbes.htm

RHINO HORNS

In traditional Chinese medicine, rhino horn is used as an aphrodisiac.

THE "TRUTH"

It's certainly true that one of the main threats to the survival of the rhino is that its so-called "horn" is used medicinally – principally to treat life-threatening fevers, and against delirium and convulsions. According to the World Wide Fund for Nature, years of investigating the trade in rhino horn has produced no evidence that it has ever been prescribed for any sexual purpose; such applications are conspicuously absent from the traditionalist's pharmacopoeia. Conservationists say that the mistrust caused by the perpetuation of this Western media myth – the cultural origins of which seem depressingly obvious – is a considerable obstacle to field work.

DISCLAIMER

If you have evidence to the contrary, please contact *FT*. It's not for us, you understand – it's for a friend.

SOURCES

www.savetherhino.org/rhinoinfo/threatstorhino/poachingfortraditionalchinesemedicine
www.salon.com/1999/09/22/medicinalanimals
www.wwf.org.uk/filelibrary/pdf/asianrhinos.pdf

BUTCH BALDIES

THE MYTH

Bald men have higher levels of testosterone than men with a full head of hair.

THE "TRUTH"

I put this belief in the same category as "Yellow teeth are stronger than white teeth" – it's a comfort myth, popular because it makes people feel better about an aspect of their appearance which doesn't conform to current beauty standards. And it suggests that the Universe observes the laws of swings-and-roundabouts justice: your shiny bonce may lessen your sexual attractiveness, but at the same time potential mates will be drawn by your heightened sexual potency, caused by all that testosterone and signalled by your baldness. But in fact, high levels of testosterone do *not* cause hair loss. Rather, men who have a genetic predisposition to male pattern baldness have hair follicles which are excessively sensitive to the sex hormone dihydrotestosterone (DHT). This causes the hair follicles to shrink, so that less hair grows and that which does is so short and fine as to be largely invisible. Tests show that on average bald and hairy men have similar levels of testosterone. It's speculated that the myth connecting baldness with potency may have arisen because castration in men halts the development of baldness, presumably by interfering with DHT production, and thus eunuchs tend to be hairy.

DISCLAIMER

Trichologists, stars of *EastEnders*, and spam-topped love machines alike, are welcome to use *FT*'s letters page to correct this column's errors, misinterpretations, and hairy howlers.

SOURCES

www.realage.com/mens-health-guide/testosterone-can-cause-hair-loss-and-baldness-in-men

http://news.consumerreports.org/health/2009/04/april-false-medical-myths-debunked.html

www.bernsteinmedical.com/hair-loss/faq-myths-more/hair-loss-myths

http://uk.askmen.com/sports/health200/222bmenshealth.html

CATHERINE'S HORSE

THE MYTH

Catherine the Great died whilst attempting sexual intercourse with her horse – either because the poor beast panicked and crushed the queen (who was strapped to its belly), or because her attendants lost their grip on the ropes which were holding it above her.

THE "TRUTH"

Respectable histories rarely mention this legend, but it's the one "fact" which most people know about Catherine (1729-96). At 15, she was married off to her mad cousin, who became Peter III of Russia. It was an unhappy (and possibly unconsummated) marriage, and in 1762 a coup resulted in Peter's death and Catherine's crowning as Empress. She began her reign as a reformer, but became one of Russia's most reactionary despots. In one matter, however, she was famously and blatantly liberal – during and after her marriage, she took many lovers. In 1796 she died in bed, following a stroke. Her sex life was the subject of much wild scurrility at home and abroad, and the bestiality tale seems to have arisen shortly after her death. Its implications are obvious: this widely despised, obese tyrant was obsessed with unladylike appetites which ruined her people and eventually cost her own life.

DISCLAIMER

This story appears to be a non-runner, but if you can mount a defence, please gallop over to the letters page.

SOURCES

The Cambridge Biographical Encyclopedia 2nd edition, edited by David Crystal (CUP, 1998)

www.nms.ac.uk/ourmuseums/nationalmuseum/exhibitions/catherinethegreat/introducingcatherine.aspx

VIRGINITY TESTS

THE MYTH

A medical examination can determine whether or not a woman is a virgin.

THE "TRUTH"

Bad news for the writers of TV crime dramas: there is no way a doctor can tell, by physical examination, whether a woman has ever had sexual intercourse. (Obviously, this doesn't exclude evidence of *recent* sexual activity, such as the presence of semen). Firstly, there's the myth of the intactness of the hymen, a leading contender for Most Misunderstood Part of the Human Body. It's widely believed (even by many dictionaries and encyclopedias) that the hymen is a solid barrier, which becomes torn asunder the first time an object (such as a penis) enters the vagina. This is nonsense; a healthy hymen has a hole in it – clearly, since otherwise it would be impossible to menstruate. A small number of women are in fact born with unbroken hymens, which have to be corrected by surgery. During adolescence, in any case, much hymenal tissue is worn away by ordinary activities such as washing, or running. In short, there is no standard state in which the hymen of a virgin or a non-virgin should present, and therefore no possible means of telling which is which. Studies have found that even when examined at magnification, using special equipment, the sexual organs of most individual women show no discernible change before and after first intercourse.

DISCLAIMER

As we never tire of pointing out, *FT* is not a medical magazine, and we are always open – wide open, even – to correction, disputation, and clarification.

SOURCES

Don't Swallow Your Gum & Other Medical Myths Debunked, Aaron Carroll & Rachel Vreeman (Penguin, 2009)

www.livescience.com/13553-5-myths-women-bodies.html

www.pamf.org/teen/health/femalehealth/hymen.html

www.psychologytoday.com/blog/all-about-sex/201103/the-hymen-membrane-widely-misunderstood

TIGHT PANTS

THE MYTH

Wearing tight underwear (or trousers) can reduce male fertility by raising the temperature of the testes, and thus lowering the sperm count.

THE "TRUTH"

More than a decade ago, in their breakout bestseller "Are boxer shorts really better? A critical analysis of the role of underwear type in male subfertility," Munkelwitz and Gilbert of the State University of New York reported, in *The Journal of Urology* (1998 Oct; 160(4):1337), their study of 97 male volunteers who had been monitored while wearing jockey or boxer shorts. The scientists found "no difference in scrotal temperature depending on underwear type." They concluded that it was "unlikely that underwear type has a significant effect on male fertility." Other studies have shown similar results, but men trying to become fathers are still routinely advised to choose the loose knickers option. It's often suggested that this belief originated in a Dutch study which showed that wearing tight leather trousers and tight plastic underwear together (but not individually) affected sperm viability. Which raises the question: how many people, even in the Netherlands, does that effect?

DISCLAIMER

Most experts argue that any temperature difference caused by tight clothes would be insufficient to make a permanent difference to sperm count, if it made any at all. Most – but not all. And even some of those who think that the idea is basically balls, nonetheless say that it *might* make a difference in borderline cases.

SOURCES

www.ncbi.nlm.nih.gov/pubmed/9751347
www.netdoctor.co.uk/menshealth/facts/semenandsperm.htm
http://ifitandhealthy.com/from-underwear-to-infertility

4. Eight glasses of water and other health hokum

Is sea air full of ozone?
Does the appendix have no function?
Does muscle turn to fat if you stop exercising?

ASBESTOS

Asbestosis, and its related cancers, is a modern plague, now defeated. Asbestos was widely used in buildings (and many everyday products) in the 1960s, and removed at great expense once its perils were understood in the 1970s and 1980s.

THE "TRUTH"

Contrary to general belief, asbestos was not suddenly discredited in the mid-to-late 20th century. In ancient Rome, it was noted that slaves working with the mineral died of lung disease. In 1889, Britain's factory inspectorate called asbestos "evil." In 1918, New York insurers refused to cover asbestos workers. Medical findings proving that asbestos workers were likely to die young were published in 1899, 1928 and 1931. The threat from non-intensive exposure has certainly been known since at least the 1960s. About 4,700 deaths a year in the UK alone are attributed to asbestos, far more in the USA, and this number is expected to continue rising until at least 2020. How can we explain our collective short-term memory loss on this matter? This column often features myths fuelled by anti-scientific paranoia; perhaps this is a rare example of one arising from a *lack* of paranoia.

DISCLAIMER

Or perhaps the whole thing's a myth, as the anti-Red Tape campaigners would have us believe. If you can help clear the air, please write in - using a lead-free pencil on unbleached paper.

SOURCES

Morning Star, 14 September 1997 and 30 June 1998

Independent on Sunday 12 December 1999

www.hse.gov.uk/statistics/causdis/asbestos.htm

OZONE

THE MYTH

Seaside air is good for you because it is full of the health-giving gas, ozone, which gives coastal areas their characteristic smell. Go on, boy, get your nose out of that book and open your lungs up!

THE "TRUTH"

The seaside doesn't smell of ozone – it smells of rotting seaweed, which releases a mixture of sulphur compounds. This is the odour which mid-Victorians mistook for ozone. Their error was great news for entrepreneurs in seaside towns; "Ozone Hotels" can still be found in Australasia. Ozone, an allotrope of oxygen, was first identified in 1840. For decades it was viewed by many medical scientists as a cure-all, which could be used in enclosed spaces, where the danger of infection was greatest, to neutralise disease-causing effluvia. Gradually, the miasma theory of disease was displaced in the consensus by the germ theory, and ozonisation fell from fashion. The myth of the ozone-rich sea breeze, however, has lived on in folklore. One thing's for certain: a good lungful of pure ozone would do your respiratory system irreparable damage.

DISCLAIMER

Research into ozone as a water cleaner, less environmentally harmful than chlorine, apparently continues – so were the Victorians right after all? And is seaside air good for you, with or without ozone? If you know, send us a saucy postcard.

SOURCES

www.abc.net.au/science/articles/2007/06/27/1963637.htm

www.telegraph.co.uk/news/uknews/1541342/Secrets-of-bracing-sea-air-bottled-by-scientists.html

EIGHT GLASSES OF WATER

Most people in the West are chronically dehydrated. For the sake of health and beauty, we should all drink eight glasses of water every day. Only pure water will do; all other drinks are dehydrating.

We do need to take in a certain amount of water daily – although no one seems to know where the eight glasses figure comes from – but we get most of it from our food. Drink lots of water, and you'll just urinate a lot. People sometimes overdose on water, with serious and occasionally fatal consequences. There's no scientific basis for the curious idea that fluids other than water (such as tea and coffee) cause dehydration. Clearly, the bottled water industry has benefited immensely from the water craze, but its origins may lie in a US National Academy of Sciences report of 1945 (or, in some accounts, a US Food and Nutrition Board report of the 1980s) which recommended 1 ml of water per calorie of food. The Board's conclusion that "most of this is contained in prepared foods" was largely overlooked in media reports. But why did this fad become an international obsession in the 2000s?

DISCLAIMER

A very small number of researchers have come forward to defend 8-ism. We would be glad to hear readers' dry data or soppy ideas; you'll find us in the pub.

SOURCES

Independent on Sunday, 20 July 2003, quoting Dr David Martin of Georgia State University, and others
Guardian, 27 January 2003, quoting Professor Heinz Valtin of Dartmouth Medical School
www.cbc.ca/news/health/story/2012/06/08/water-eight-glasses-myth.html

for
HEALTH & BEAUTY

HUNT EMERSON
RECOMMENDS
8 GLASSES OF WATER
PER DAY

THE APPENDIX

THE MYTH

The human appendix has no function. It may have had one in our evolutionary past, but today is merely a vestigial organ - often fatal when infected, but otherwise of no significance.

THE "TRUTH"

Scientists are still debating what, precisely, is or are the function or functions of the appendix - but you won't find many who still think it doesn't have any. The puzzle, of course, is that when the appendix is removed, no harm befalls the patient. Two current theories seem to explain this. One is that the appendix acts as a factory and/or a safe haven for beneficial gut bacteria; modern humans, living in high population densities, can easily obtain such bacteria from each other. The more conventional view is that the appendix produces endocrine cells in foetuses, and antibodies and white blood cells in young adults. However, because it is not the only source of such necessaries, the appendix is - while far from functionless - not actually essential to the well-being of the modern human.

DISCLAIMER

In the uniquely strange world of US scientific debate, this matter is surprisingly controversial: creationist teachers use the supposed anomaly of the appendix as an argument against the theory of evolution, and are reluctant to see it lose that particular function. Feel free to dispute any of the above, via the letters column - with footnotes, if required.

SOURCES

www.abc.net.au/news/stories/2007/10/10/2055374.htm
http://amos.indiana.edu/library/scripts/appendix.html
http://blogs.scientificamerican.com/guest-blog/2012/01/02/your-appendix-could-save-your-life/

BOOZE AND PILLS

You mustn't drink alcohol while you're on antibiotics. If you do, you'll get ill, or the antis won't work, or both.

THE "TRUTH"

In general, there is no reason at all to give up booze while on a course of antibiotics. Check with your pharmacist before heading for the off-license, because there are a few, specific antis which could cause side-effects if mixed with alcohol. But the widespread advice to avoid the cocktail at all times has no basis whatsoever in pharmacology. Some medical historians suggest an intriguing origin for this myth. In the early days of penicillin being used to treat VD, doctors – especially those attached to the armed forces – spotted a perfect opportunity to limit the harm done to their patients by excessive drinking, if only for the duration of the antibiotic course. At the same time, keeping the patient sober might just prevent him from passing on his infection before the drugs took effect. In other words, the "don't drink" mythconception may have its origins in deliberate misinformation, motivated by a pragmatic approach to preventative medicine.

DISCLAIMER

It's a pretty good rule in life not to base important decisions concerning medical matters on things you read in magazine columns, no matter how nicely illustrated. Corrections, and additions, to any of the above should be written illegibly in Latin and sent to the letters page.

SOURCES

www.dailymail.co.uk/health/article-566058/We-expose-truth-age-old-health-myths.html
www.abc.net.au/dimensions/dimensions_health/Transcripts/s776185.htm
www.nhs.uk/chq/pages/871.aspx?categoryid=73&subcategoryid=103

GROUND GLASS

THE MYTH

Ground glass is a deadly poison.

THE "TRUTH"

Finely powdered glass has long been claimed as a method of both murder and manslaughter, when secreted in food or used to adulterate substances such as recreational drugs, but this belief was debunked as long ago as 1642 - when physician Sir Thomas Browne wrote: "That Glass is poison, according unto common conceit, I know not how to grant... from experience, as having given unto Dogs above a dram thereof, subtilly powdered in Butter and Paste, without any visible disturbance" - and frequently since. The key point is simply that in order to be large enough to cause even minor internal injury, the fragments of glass would need to be so big as to be impossible not to notice in the mouth. Powdered, glass is harmless.

DISCLAIMER

"One does not dispose of a belief by showing that it is irrational," noted George Orwell, and I for one shall continue to be amongst those who shun ground glass as a foodstuff. Meanwhile, any innardologist who can refute the refutations of this story should air his gripes on *FT*'s letters pages.

SOURCES

www.abc.net.au/science/k2/moments/s1828923.htm

Murder & Mayhem: A Doctor Answers Medical and Forensic Questions for Mystery Writers, DP Lyle (St Martin's, 2003)

DEADLY FLIES

THE MYTH

Houseflies spread disease by traipsing dung all over our food.

THE "TRUTH"

Despite an immense and varied industry devoted to protecting us from the deadly housefly, the fact is that if you live in Britain, your precautions are probably unnecessary. There are two kinds of housefly: *Musca domestica* and *Fannia canicularis*. *Musca* is no longer common in the UK, except in rural areas where there are plenty of manure heaps in which it can breed. It used to be our main housefly, and is indeed a notorious spreader of a wide range of pathogens, but its sad decline began when motor vehicles started to replace horses; cars don't crap. In most of the UK, the muscid you're likely to encounter is *Fannia*. This is the fellow seen flying triangular patterns underneath hanging lightbulbs, and is not linked with disease, having, unlike its cousin, no interest in human food.

DISCLAIMER

If you happen to be in a country still hymned for its bucolic charms – such as France – please note that *M. domestica* continues its dirty work in such places with never-dimmed enthusiasm. Meanwhile, if your data clash with ours, you're invited to rub your legs all over our letters pages.

SOURCES

BBC Wildlife magazine, November 2009

Correspondence with Dr Peter C Barnard, Director of Science at The Royal Entomological Society

FROM MUSCLE TO FAT

THE MYTH

If you build up a lot of muscle through exercise, and then become more sedentary in your habits, the muscle will turn into fat – which is why you see so many jellified ex-athletes.

THE "TRUTH"

It is physically impossible for muscle to "turn into" fat – they are made from two different types of cell. For muscle to become fat (or, indeed, for fat to become muscle, through exercise) would be like turnips turning into ball bearings. Muscle cells and fat cells perform different functions, and work in different ways. When you reduce the amount of exercise your skeletal muscles are receiving, they shrink. When you increase the amount of exercise, they grow. Similarly, fat cells expand or contract according to the amount of food they are given. The reason that so many retired sportsmen look flabby or overweight is not that their formerly impressive musculature has undergone magical transformation which has caused it to melt into fat; it's almost certainly because during their sporting careers they became used to needing to eat large amounts, and have not subsequently reduced their daily calorie intake in line with the reduction in their physical activity. (Plus, of course, commentary boxes are notorious cake-magnets.)

DISCLAIMER

The experts are pretty unequivocal about this, but, as ever, if you know better, you are invited to exercise your right to reply via the letters page.

SOURCES

www.abc.net.au/science/articles/2006/05/01/1613539.htm

http://articles.chicagotribune.com/2011-09-28/health/sc-health-0928-fitness-myths-201109281fitness-myths-muscle-cells

5. Viking helmets and other historical nonsense

Did Vikings wear horned helmets?
Were people smaller in the old days?
Did Mussolini make the trains run on time?

RUGBY BALLS

THE MYTH

Rugby Football was invented in November 1823, at Rugby School, when 17-year-old player William Webb Ellis - "with a fine disregard for the rules" - first picked up a ball and ran with it.

THE "TRUTH"

Various forms of football were played in many countries before codification began in Britain in the 19th century. In Ellis's time, each major English public school stuck to its own version, and inter-school matches were unknown. However, handling the ball was common to most forms of the game, until eventually banned from what became soccer in 1863. The Rugby Football Union was formed in 1871, its clubs drawn mostly from the London area. There's no doubt that the anomalous Rugby game has its modern roots in the eponymous school, but Ellis's involvement is entirely apocryphal. The story appeared for the first time in 1875 (Ellis having died in 1872) in an article in the school magazine, and no evidence to support it was offered at the time or has ever emerged since. It seems likely that Ellis himself died quite unaware of his supposed role in sporting history.

DISCLAIMER

But there's a statue in Rugby of Ellis inventing the game, and a plaque commemorating his act at the school. Surely stone cannot lie? If you'd like to refute the debunking, or at least try (*officially sanctioned rugby pun*), please run as fast as you can to *FT*'s letters page.

SOURCES

www.rugbyfootballhistory.com; www.pshortell.demon.co.uk/rugby/ch3.htm
www.rfu.com/twickenhamstadium/worldrugbymuseum/rugbyhistory/howfootballbecamerugby
The Daily Telegraph A to Z of Sport, Trevor Montague (Little Brown, 2004)

SLAVERY

THE MYTH

Slavery was abolished in Britain in 1807 (or 1833, or 1834).

THE "TRUTH"

Holding a person in slavery became illegal in the UK on 6 April 2010. Nineteenth century legislation made slavery illegal, in stages, throughout the British Empire, but the status of "slave" had never existed under English common law. Therefore, since slaves did not legally exist in this country, holding a slave was never made specifically illegal – until 2010. Section 71 of the Coroners and Justice Act 2009 makes it an offence in the UK to hold a person in slavery or servitude, or require a person to perform forced or compulsory labour. The maximum penalties are 7 and 14 years imprisonment respectively. Is this just pedantry? Not according to modern anti-slavery campaigners, who say that there are currently 27 million slaves worldwide, in various categories, and that the use of undocumented migrants as forced labour is common in Britain. They argue that it's only in countries where slavery has been *criminalised*, as opposed to merely *abolished*, that the prosecution of slaveholders becomes practical.

DISCLAIMER

This is a complicated matter, and if we've got any of it wrong, we order you to write in and tell us.

SOURCES

Correspondence with the pressure group Anti-Slavery International
www.morningstaronline.co.uk/index.php/news/content/view/full/82855
www.legislation.gov.uk/ukpga/2009/25/notes/contents
www.anti-slaverysociety.addr.com/huk-1833act.htm
www.antislavery.org/english

VIKING HELMETS

THE MYTH

Vikings wore hats with horns on.

THE "TRUTH"

They didn't. Eddie Grundy from *The Archers* does own a horned hat, but the Vikings never did. The foremost academic expert on the non-existent lids, Dr Roberta Frank of Yale University, author of *The Invention of the Viking Horned Helmet* (2000), speaking on BBC Radio 4, was unequivocal: the Vikings "never, ever got near such a thing." Indeed, it's hard to imagine why anyone *would* wear headgear with handles on when going into a hand-to-hand battle. It's generally thought that Viking warriors wore, if anything, simple leather helmets. Dr Frank blames the horns' popularity on Carl Emil Doepler, costume designer for the original 1876 production of Wagner's *Ring*. Instructed by Wagner to scour Danish and Swedish museums for inspiration, Doepler seems to have been a little casual with his historical precision; he might have been confused by the horned (but non-Viking) figure which appears on the Gundestrup Cauldron.

DISCLAIMER

Some evidence for ancient horned helmets does exist, but it's believed they were only used ceremonially and had gone out of fashion before the Viking age. But if you can give the Viking horns a pre-Wagnerian origin, please yell.

SOURCES

The Viking Way, BBC Radio 4, 2 November 2005

Sunday Telegraph, 6 November 2005

TITCHY ANCESTORS

THE MYTH

People were much smaller in the old days.

THE "TRUTH"

I can't remember when I last met a teenager who wasn't taller than his or her parents, which makes the persistence of this modern myth easy to understand. But the two things all informed sources seem to agree on are that average height rises *and falls* over the centuries – and that it doesn't rise or fall by all that much. Figures abound, based on the excavations of dated skeletons; the "average mediaeval man" in Britain was 1.71 metres tall; a mere 4cm (in some reports, 2cm) shorter than a modern Briton. Saxon Londoners were "similar in height" to today's, but Roman Londoners were "6cm shorter." Hunter-gatherers, some claim, were taller than we are. Some experts argue that average height in Britain fell in the 19th (some say 18th) century, as the industrial revolution impoverished millions, leading to poor diets, long working hours, child labour, and other height-suppressant factors. Early health and safety legislation, and better nutrition following the repeal of the Corn Laws, then saw the average go up again; in other words, the rise of trade unionism leads to the rising of the race. But this is by no means universally accepted.

DISCLAIMER

I'm no expert, but I wonder – how significant are the sample sizes? And, since differences in average height seem to be largely determined by social class, how statistically valid are studies based on remains if the status of the deceased is unknown? If you can add anything to this debate, other than tall stories, please write to us.

SOURCES

www.museumoflondon.org.uk/archive/exhibits/bodies/bodies.htm
www.museumoflondon.org.uk/Collections-Research/Research/Your-Research/Londinium/analysis/romanlondoners/appearance/12+Tall.htm
http://www.economist.com/node/17722650

I STARTED SO I'LL FINISH

The Air Raid Warden who "started" World War Two by sounding Britain's first air raid siren was also the man who "ended" the war, by sounding the final All Clear.

THE "TRUTH"

This is surely one of the best-known, and most pleasingly neat of all "symmetrical history" myths. Sadly, it's not true – according to the man himself. Frank Buckley was indeed "the first to hit the red button," at 11.15am on 3 September 1939, when he was a civil defence officer on duty at a fire station in Bristol. As the Prime Minister broadcast from London, announcing the war against Germany, "the telephone rang with an 'air raid warning red' from the Royal Observer Corps." It was a false alarm. Sixty years after his moment of immortality, the then 85-year-old former barrister told a reporter: "There was some talk of me being the person to sound the last all-clear when the war ended, but it never happened in all the celebrations." Presumably, that unfulfilled intention is the origin of the story. Nonetheless, Mr Buckley is apparently immortalised as the figure of an ARP warden on a stained glass window in Bristol Cathedral.

DISCLAIMER

It's not often we get a mythconception debunked by its central character, so I suppose we must accept this as the final word. Of course, if you can prove otherwise, then please contact us by carrier pigeon.

SOURCES

www.thefreelibrary.com/I+STARTED+THE+WAR%3B+Frank+sounded+first+raid+siren.-a060409273

THE PHILISTINES

THE MYTH

Long ago, there lived a race of boors so devoid of enlightenment, finer feelings, and aesthetic development that, centuries later, their name – Philistine – is still used as a byword for anyone who lacks an interest in or understanding of the arts.

THE "TRUTH"

This is what we get for never reading *Brewer's*, or indeed any ordinary English dictionary, from cover to cover, for the pejorative in question has only the faintest connection with ancient inhabitants of south-west Palestine. A misunderstood Biblical quotation seems to have led to the term *Philister* being applied by 17th century German university students to the common townspeople – an example of the "Town and Gown" snobbery well-known throughout the academic world. From Germany, the libel travelled to America, and thence to Britain in the early or mid-19th century. Presumably, the popular idea that the Philistines had no indigenous culture was simply a case of "back formation," as people attempted to provide a historical explanation for the neologism.

DISCLAIMER

Before the descendants of the Philistines send for the spin doctors, it's worth wondering why this calumny was so readily accepted. Is there any evidence in history or legend to support it? We'd be delighted to hear from any readers who actually know how to read and write.

SOURCES

Independent, 21 July 1999
Brewer's Dictionary of Phrase and Fable, 14th Edition

ELLIS ISLAND

THE MYTH

Immigrants to the USA between the 1890s and 1940s, arriving at Ellis Island in New York, often had their names changed to make them sound more "American".

THE "TRUTH"

This widely believed (and widely resented) story seems to have no truth in it whatsoever, according to everyone who has ever researched it. Passengers arriving as immigrants would appear on ships' manifests before they left their port of departure. The accuracy of these lists would be attested to by ships' officers, and then checked in the US by immigration officials. Interpreters were available to ensure that "difficult" names were recorded correctly. Of course, some errors must have occurred, but this would have happened during the naturalisation process, and not at Ellis Island. Similarly, some immigrants chose to change their names for various reasons, but comparison of arrival records with naturalisation documents and city directories shows that this usually happened some time after arrival. Researchers are adamant: no one ever had their name changed at Ellis Island.

DISCLAIMER

Many US immigrants and their descendants still insist that they owe their ethnically-cleansed surnames to the Island's officials. Are they all the victims of folkloric delusions – or of a gap between bureaucratic theory and practice? As ever, we welcome contributions to this debate from readers, whether or not their monickers match our records.

SOURCES

www.genealogy.com/88donna.html
www.ilw.com/articles/2005,0808-smith.shtm

MUSSOLINI'S RAILWAYS

THE MYTH

When Benito Mussolini seized power in Italy in 1922, his first great achievement was to impose order on the nation's chaotic rail system.

THE "TRUTH"

Cavaliere Carlo Crova, general manager of the State Railways during the 1920s, greatly improved the network's performance. However, much of his reform and repair programme was carried out before the Fascists came to power; that it was completed during Mussolini's reign is a coincidence, which Musso hijacked to demonstrate the effectiveness of Fascist methods. In fact, most historians now suggest that the trains under the dictator were *not* particularly efficient – but that Fascist spin-doctoring was, aided by a pathetically compliant international press corps. The phrase "At least Mussolini made the trains run on time" is as popular as ever today, with those who wish to damn their own governments as useless, even in comparison with despised regimes, or to argue that one success does not outweigh many crimes or failures, or (increasingly, these days) to suggest that Fascism may be a bit rough, but it gets things done.

DISCLAIMER

If any elderly Italian trainspotters would like to share their 1920s notebooks with us, we will meet you under the clock at noon. Or you could just write in.

SOURCES

www.independent.co.uk/voices/rear-window-making-italy-work-did-mussolini-really-get-the-trains-running-on-time-1367688.html

www.independent.co.uk/arts-entertainment/letter-mussolini-myth-1100011.html

6. The tongue map and other fables of food

Does turkey make you drowsy?
Does Coke dissolve your teeth overnight?
Does chewing gum get tangled in your insides?

THE TONGUE MAP

Humans experience each of the different tastes on different parts of the tongue.

You can still find "Tongue Maps" in books and on websites today, showing that sweet is tasted on the tip of the tongue, bitter at the back, and so on. You can even buy special sets of dedicated wineglasses, individually designed to channel the dominant flavours of different wines to the appropriate areas of the tongue. But it's been known for a long time that all tastes can be detected wherever there are taste buds. Regular readers of this column will be unsurprised to learn that it's all a historic misunderstanding. Early in the 20th century, studies showed that the tongue has zones of *relative sensitivity* to the different tastes – and ever since, that's been misinterpreted as meaning that they could only be tasted in one zone each. In 1974, a scientist named Virginia Collings re-examined the theory, and found that sensitivity to the main tastes did vary around the tongue – but only insignificantly, and to a degree which is unnoticeable under normal conditions.

DISCLAIMER

No doubt the orthodoxy on this matter will change again one day, as orthodoxies do, but the idea of the rigidly demarcated tongue is easily shown to be false by simply putting some sugar on the part of your tongue which the map says tastes only salt.

SOURCES

www.aromadictionary.com/articles/tonguemaparticle.html

www.livescience.com/7113-tongue-map-tasteless-myth-debunked.html

http://blog.wineenthusiast.com/2008/03/31/a-little-clarity-on-wine-glasses/

TUTANKHAMEN'S PEAS

THE MYTH

Dried peas discovered in Tutankhamen's tomb in 1922 were found to be viable; the variety called Tutankhamen's Pea, commercially available today, is descended from those ancient seeds.

THE "TRUTH"

There are a number of varieties of "Mummy's Peas"(and, indeed, sweet peas) on sale today, but the seed heritage experts at Kew Gardens say that "To the best of our knowledge, none of these stories is strongly supported by archaeological evidence." Various sources point out that the conditions in tombs, which have ensured the survival of many artefacts, are in fact too dry for good seed storage. Other than uncorroborated tradition, there seems to be no evidence that any seeds found in ancient Egyptian tombs have ever been successfully germinated. It's widely claimed that in the 19th and early 20th centuries, at the height of the Western craze for Egyptology, local entrepreneurs were happy to sell to tourists ordinary, modern seeds, represented as having been recovered from tombs. A simple misunderstanding may also be involved; it is sometimes said that Tutankhamen's Pea originated on the country estate of Lord Caernarvon, who financed Howard Carter's search for King Tut's resting place – and was subsequently named in honour of Carenarvon's claim to fame, rather than the plant's origin.

DISCLAIMER

The mundane explanations – either crooked or confused or both – seem the more likely. But the story is undeniably incomplete, so if you have proof that it's wrong, please wrap it up in bandages, and send it lurching towards our letters column.

SOURCES

www.kew.org/science-conservation/save-seed-prosper/millennium-seed-bank/ask-the-msb/faq/seeds-live/index.htm
The Seed Savers' Handbook, Cherfas, Fanton & Fanton (Grover Books, 1996)
www.seeds.ca/info/sod/seedexchange.php
Seed News, Autumn 2005
http://chestofbooks.com/gardening-horticulture/Gardener-Monthly-V27/Mummy-Peas.html

TURKEY DROWSY

THE MYTH

The reason you fall asleep after a traditional Christmas (or, in the US, Thanksgiving) turkey dinner is that the meat contains a natural sedative, called tryptophan.

THE "TRUTH"

Many people *do* become sleepy after feasting on turkey, and turkey *does* contain tryptophan. However, there is no connection between these two facts – despite this being the one thing every US resident knows about Thanksgiving. Tryptophan is an amino acid, essential to human health, and found in a wide range of animal and vegetable foods. Turkey corpses are a good, though by no means unusually rich, source; soya beans, for instance, contain much higher levels. Our bodies use tryptophan to produce serotonin, which (amongst other functions) helps us sleep. Indeed, tryptophan has been used pharmaceutically as a treatment for insomnia. But to get that sort of effect, you'd need to take it in high doses, on an empty stomach, and "undiluted" by other amino acids. It is simply impossible for tryptophan, as an ingredient in a foodstuff, to cause immediate drowsiness or sleep. There are various possible causes of "Turkey Drowsy," such as the tendency for festive meals to be much larger than usual, to involve more alcohol, and to include unaccustomed quantities of carbohydrate-rich vegetables; these release insulin, which makes the tryptophan already stored in your body more effective.

DISCLAIMER

Of course, the *real* reason we fall asleep after Xmas Dinner is to avoid having to converse with our relatives. But if you can add to, or correct, any of the gourmet morsels in this banquet of gastro-science, please serve your platter on our letters pages.

SOURCES

http://news.nationalgeographic.com/news/2005/11/1122051122thanksgiving.htm
http://www.bidmc.org/YourHealth/HolisticHealth/HealthMythsCenter.aspx?ChunkID=156999

CAMEMBERT

THE MYTH

Camembert cheese was invented in 1791, in the village of the same name, by milkmaid Marie Harel. As the Terror raged across France, Marie bravely (or treacherously, depending on your POV) gave shelter to a recusant priest from Brie, the Abbé Bonvoust (or Gobert, in some versions). In return, he taught her the secret process which made Brie cheese unique. By combining Brie techniques with an existing local cheese, Marie created democratic France's national cheese - a revolutionary mixture of old and new.

THE "TRUTH"

The priest never existed, say historians; Marie Harel didn't live in Camembert at the time; and there are published mentions of Camembert cheese - or, at least, of a Camembert cheese - dating back to the 1680s. The legend of Marie seems to have become popular only in the 1920s, when a grateful American, who believed the cheese had cured his digestive troubles, began a fund to erect a statue to the mythical milkmaid. Scholars suggest that the tale of Marie and the priest served to strengthen the brand identity both of the cheese, and the nation itself. In reality, Camembert probably owes its global fame to the invention at the end of the 19th century of the characteristic little wooden box which allowed the cheese to travel safely by rail.

DISCLAIMER

The "traditional" story still has its defenders. If you'd like to whey the evidence and tell us what you think really o'curd, please write in.

SOURCES

www.taste-camembert.com/en/camembert-history.php
www.guardian.co.uk/books/2003/dec/01/londonreviewofbooks
Economist, 26 July 2003

CHEWING GUM

THE MYTH

Chewing gum is inedible, so if you swallow it, it will get tangled up in your innards. This can have harmful – even fatal – consequences for the digestive system.

THE "TRUTH"

Nobody ever said exposing mythconceptions was going to be easy. It involves rigorous scepticism – even to the extreme extent of sometimes not believing what your mum told you when you were little. Chewing gum is, indeed, inedible in the sense that it cannot be digested, but it won't stick to the walls of your stomach, which are moist and slippery. Instead, it will pass straight through the system (and having done so, can presumably be retrieved and re-used – though perhaps not in America, where it is a Well Known Fact that gum stays in your guts for seven years). However, *habitual* swallowing of gum might be ill-advised, according to a handful of reports from surgeons of children suffering blockages from eating extreme amounts of the stuff. A related story in the US has it that bubble-gum ice cream was banned for a time during the 1970s, after a child choked and died on it.

DISCLAIMER

It's widely assumed that this bit of medical scaremongering was started by gum-hating parents, though I think it just as likely that it came from the ghastly imaginations of horrible little children. Either way, we claim no special expertise in the fields of Gumology or Innardsism, and would be happy to hear further evidence from readers who've chewed the matter over.

SOURCES

Independent, 9 February 2001

www.scientificamerican.com/article.cfm?id=fact-or-fiction-chewing-gum-takes-seven-years-to-digest

THE COKE SMILE

THE MYTH

A tooth left in a glass of Coca-Cola overnight will have vanished by morning – dissolved in the vile drink's mighty acids. (In some versions, the disappearing object is a fly, a coin or an iron nail).

THE "TRUTH"

For once, we have here a myth with a solid origin. In 1950, Professor Clive McCay of Cornell University told a select committee of the US House of Representatives that the high levels of sugar and phosphoric acid in Coke caused tooth decay. To illustrate his testimony, he said that a tooth left in a glass of Coke would begin to dissolve after two days. Even if McCay's claim were accurate (those who have tried the experiment say it's not), it is in any case irrelevant: nobody holds cola in their mouths for two days, not even people who actually *like* the taste of badger sweat, and the acids it contains are dealt with by the digestive system. Many common foods are more acidic than Coke. Of course, it's generally agreed that soft drinks can cause tooth decay, but they do so gradually. Nonetheless, the tooth-in-Coke story is still widely believed – perhaps because of its impressive provenance.

DISCLAIMER

If you've successfully dissolved one of your Hampsteads in the manner described then, obviously, feel free to disregard the above. But please, when the pain killers wear off, let us have the details.

SOURCES

http://whyfiles.org/129scifable/3.html; http://healthyliving.msn.com/nutrition/cokelore-coke-facts-and-myths-impacting-health-1

MEDIAEVAL GRUB

THE MYTH

Cooks in the Middle Ages heavily spiced their food in order to disguise the taste of rancid meat.

THE "TRUTH"

Though widely unquestioned, this is one of those beliefs which shrivels as soon as it's exposed to light. Spices might hide the taste of rotten meat, but they wouldn't protect against food poisoning. Exotic flavourings were expensive status symbols, and anyone who could afford to use spices liberally could also afford fresh meat. In any case, mediaeval people knew a great deal about keeping food fresh, and used various techniques of preservation, such as salting and pickling. Animal carcasses did not travel many food miles in those days; slaughtering was done locally, and records show that meat hygiene laws were strictly enforced. It's also worth noting that spicy food went out of fashion in the British Isles centuries before the invention of refrigeration – and became popular again at a time when fridges were universally available.

DISCLAIMER

If you remember getting ill after dining at a mediaeval lord's table, please report the matter to your local trading standards office; if your knowledge of this subject is greater than ours, please write to our letters page.

SOURCES

http://public.wsu.edu/~delahoyd/medieval/medievalfood.html
http://historymedren.about.com/od/misconceptions/a/rottenmeat.htm

TASTEBUD MASSACRE

THE MYTH

Very spicy food – specifically, that which gets its "heat" from capsicums – destroys taste buds.

THE "TRUTH"

Capsaicin, the active ingredient in chilli peppers, causes numbness in the mouth; this is because, for unknown reasons, the nerve endings react to capsaicin as if it were heat. To protect you from the pain of being burned, your brain blocks the sensation, which you experience as temporary and localised numbness. How temporary and how local, of course, depends on how piquant the food is, but the key word is *temporary*. And this is true no matter how extreme the spiciness of the chilli; a gobfull of ultra-hot peppers, eaten raw, might leave you numb-tongued for many hours, but you will regain the full range of feeling in your mouth sooner or later. Although your sense of taste is limited for the duration, which may make you feel as if your taste buds have been destroyed, no permanent damage is done, or can be done. It is true that we lose much of our ability to taste during the course of our lives, but that's just senescence. Taste bud cells die off and are replaced all the time, but not eternally; eventually, they die and are not replaced. The spiciness or blandness of your diet over the years will have no effect on the subtlety of your palate in old age.

DISCLAIMER

All sources for this seem to refer back to a single study; not always a good sign in the de-mything business. If the arguments taste wrong to you, please let us know.

SOURCES

http://news.yahoo.com/myth-debunked-spicy-food-doesnt-really-kill-taste-190810067.html

7. Nelson's eyepatch and other famous myths about famous people

Was Hitler a vegetarian?
Was Queen Elizabeth I bald?
Did King Canute order the tide to turn back?

HITLER THE VEGETARIAN

THE MYTH

Adolf Hitler was a vegetarian. While the British parliament debated the abolition of blood sports in 1998, the *Daily Telegraph* responded with an article explaining that the Nazis were not only vegetarians, but fanatical supporters of animal rights in general – and that Nazism and vegetarianism were psychologically linked. Just in case this was too subtle a message, it was accompanied by a cartoon showing Hitler standing outside a concentration camp, cuddling a fox. Yup, right – got it now.

THE "TRUTH"

It's easy to understand the attractions of this myth; how better to dramatise the accusation that vegetarians "care more for animals than for humans" than by painting the 20th century's premier incarnation of evil as a sentimental monster? But Herr Hitler, dictator of Germany 1933-45, was not a vegetarian. What he was, was a farter; he suffered from chronic flatulence, a completely unamusing medical condition, and for this reason frequently went on a vegetarian (or vegetarian-ish) diet – a remedy which will surprise many vegetarians.

Some historians suggest Nazi Party PR deliberately created an image of their leader as an ascetic, shunning tobacco, alcohol, romance and red meat in favour of a life devoted entirely to serving his nation. Various biographers and memoirists, including those who knew the dictator intimately, record his passion for Bavarian sausages, game pie, and in particular a delicacy known as stuffed squab, made from baby pigeons. In 2008, a Belgian TV series about famous people's favourite dishes filmed an episode concerning Hitler's passion for trout in butter sauce. The show was cancelled, following protests from concentration camp survivors.

If Hitler had been a committed vegetarian, it's reasonable to suppose that vegetarianism would have been the in-thing amongst Nazi sycophants. Not only was there never such a craze, but vegetarian societies and journals were banned, along with other "internationalist" groups such as Esperanto clubs.

This was the first ever Mythconception, and it continues to be perhaps the most controversial. For a long time this puzzled me, but over the years I think I've come to understand the problem. To vegetarians, Hitler was clearly not a vegetarian *because he ate meat*. To a vegetarian, not eating meat is what "vegetarian" means. However, to many meat-eaters, vegetarian is defined more loosely; it can mean, for instance, someone who avoids certain meats, or who deliberately reduces their overall meat consumption, in pursuit of some imagined health benefit. One 1930s feature writer depicted Hitler, without irony, as a keen vegetarian who was fond of ham and caviar. Hence the inability of the two sides of this argument to agree; they are using different dictionaries. As ever, though, we would be pleased to hear from anyone who has facts to add.

SOURCES

Daily Telegraph, 17 January 1998

Daily Telegraph, 29 October 2008

http://intellectualyst.com/mein-salad-on-hitlers-not-being-a-vegetarian

The Australian Vegetarian, November/December 1989

The Realeat Encyclopaedia of Vegetarian Living, Peter Cox (Bloomsbury, 1994)

www.vegsource.com/berry/hitler.html

WC FIELDS'S GRAVESTONE

THE MYTH

The gravestone of comic actor WC Fields is inscribed "On the whole, I'd sooner be in Philadelphia."

THE "TRUTH"

It's perhaps the most famous bequeathed giggle of all time: the monumental engraving which marks the final rotting place of a man who is remembered and revered as much for his misanthropy as for the films he appeared in. It hurts me to type these words, but – folks, there is no such tombstone message. There isn't even a tombstone. WC was cremated, and the plaque upon his reliquary carries only the simple, restrained, and hideously disappointing words: "WC Fields 1880-1946".

DISCLAIMER

What a revoltin' development! Can anyone say it ain't so? Mythcon Control would be unusually pleased to hear from you, if you can disprove this piece of po-faced revisionism.

SOURCES

Independent, 30 January 1999, quoting *Man on the Flying Trapeze: The Life and Times of WC Fields*, Simon Louvish (Faber, 1999)

KING CANUTE

THE MYTH

King Canute (or Knut, or possibly Cnut the Great, if you're confident of your typing skills) was a vain and foolish king, a megalomaniac who tried to demonstrate his power by ordering the tide to turn back.

THE "TRUTH"

Son of Sweyn Forkbeard, Canute was King of England 1016-35. Historians admire him as a reformer and peace-bringer. The story has it that, tired of his courtiers' flattery, he had them witness his unsuccessful attempts to command the sea – his point being that, however powerful a man may be, he is yet a mortal, and not a god. The story first appeared in the 12th century *Historia Anglorum*, in which Henry of Huntingdon has Canute declaim: "Let all the world know that the power of kings is empty and worthless and there is no King worthy of the name save Him by whose will heaven and earth and sea obey eternal laws." Interestingly, this is one case where the "myth" and the "truth" both carry the same moral. This is what you might call a cockroach myth – it staggers on, no matter how often it's stamped on. It still crops up with astonishing frequency in newspaper reports and broadcasts.

DISCLAIMER

Ah, but, is either version true, or was the whole thing a piece of posthumous PR? If you know more, please send us a message in a bottle.

SOURCES

www.bbc.co.uk/news/magazine-13524677

A Dictionary of British History, edited by JP Kenyon (Secker & Warburg, 1981)

BESSIE SMITH'S NEEDLESS DEATH

THE MYTH

In September 1937, the black blues singer Bessie Smith was involved in a car crash in Mississippi. Her injuries should not have been fatal, but she died of blood loss after being refused admission to a hospital reserved for whites. This story has been known to generations of Americans, but is also very popular in other countries as an example of the evils both of apartheid and of non-socialised medicine. Occasionally the subject of the legend is not Smith, but some other prominent black entertainer.

THE "TRUTH"

Music historians today seem to be agreed that Smith was taken directly to Clarksdale's black hospital immediately following her accident, but within weeks of her death, *Down Beat* magazine carried an article headlined "Did Bessie Smith bleed to death while waiting for medical aid?". In 1957, the same publication ran a piece debunking its own myth, but in 1960 Edward Albee's play *The Death of Bessie Smith* reinforced the segregation version.

DISCLAIMER

FT never claims to know the last word on a truth, or to finally bury a myth. If you can tell us more about the dying hours of this great American artist, please do.

SOURCES

http://womenshistory.about.com/library/pic/blpbessiesmith001.htm
Correspondence with readers, drawing on the book *Bessie* by Chris Albertson (Stein & Day, 1972)

NELSON'S EYE PATCH

THE MYTH

Admiral Nelson wore a patch over his right eye-socket, to hide the disfigured (or missing) eyeball.

THE "TRUTH"

Nelson never wore an eye-patch. The nearest he came to it was a peaked eye-shade which he had built onto his naval hat, but that was there to protect his good eye from the sun, not to hide his bad eye. Horatio was awarded a disability allowance for his missing right arm (mislaid during the battle of Santa Cruz), but the Navy refused him one for his blinded eye, because their doctors couldn't tell whether it was genuinely sightless. In other words, Nelson had no need to wear an eye-patch, because there was no disfigurement to hide. Have a look at Nelson's Column: no eye-patch. There are no patches, either, on any portrait made during his lifetime. The little black number seems to have been invented in the mid-19th century, perhaps to accentuate the great man's disabilities, and therefore his heroism. The image was cemented in 1941, when Laurence Olivier played a patched-up Nelson in the film *That Hamilton Woman*.

DISCLAIMER

This column expects every reader to do his duty; if you can prove the patch, send us a signal.

SOURCES

www.bbc.co.uk/history/british/empireseapower/nelson01.shtml
www.telegraph.co.uk/news/1481516/Nelson-didnt-wear-eye-patch-says-historian.html

BALD LIZ

Queen Elizabeth I was bald at the age of thirty.

THE "TRUTH"

When I was at school, we were taught that Elizabeth went bald because she used arsenic-based make-up. Today, the more common story is that a bad case of smallpox left her hairless. Either way, there seems no reason to believe that she actually was slap-headed, either as a young woman or an old one, other than the fact that she wore wigs – which were, after all, common enough in the fashions of her time. A lock of greying hair, supposedly the Queen's, and dated to either 1572 or 1582, is still extant at Wilton House near Salisbury. There are contemporary references to her hair as late as 1599, when she was in her mid-60s. Liz biographer Elizabeth Jenkins dates the baldness story to a mistaken belief, by a writer in the 1920s, that no portrait of the queen after 1564 showed her with hair; by 1931, this had become Hilaire Belloc's unadorned and unsupported statement, in an edition of his *History of England*, that "At 30 she was as bald as an egg."

DISCLAIMER

Neither the hirsute not the shiny-pated camps appear to be in possession of absolute proof, so if you have evidence either way, don't keep it under your hat – send it to our letters page.

SOURCES
Elizabeth the Great, Elizabeth Jenkins (Artus Books, 2001)
www.elizabethi.org/uk/myths/
http://collections.vam.ac.uk/item/O16414/portrait-miniature-hilliard-nicholas/
www.bbc.co.uk/history/british/tudors/elizabeth_i_01.shtml#four

VICTORIA AND THE FAMINE

THE MYTH

During what the British generally call "The Irish Potato Famine" of the 1840s and 50s, when a million died and perhaps two million were forced to emigrate, Queen Victoria demonstrated her contempt for their suffering by donating £5 to famine relief – and on the same day giving £10 to Battersea Dogs Home. Almost unknown in Britain, this story is widely believed in Ireland, and amongst the Irish diaspora.

THE "TRUTH"

Battersea Dogs Home was founded in 1860, so that seems to deal with that aspect of the tale. Whether the Queen was a supporter of earlier canine charities I don't know – but what *is* certain is that she was the world's largest single donor to Irish famine relief, giving £2,000 in January 1847. In March that year, she sent out a Queen's Letter calling for donations, which raised the enormous sum of £170,571. Significantly, a second Letter, in October, brought in just £30,167. The Queen's more sympathetic view had by now lost out to elements in the Establishment which saw the need to defend the laissez-faire principle of non-intervention at any cost, and to moralists who argued that famine was God's way of teaching the Irish to be less "feckless."

DISCLAIMER

The continuing debate amongst historians over whether the starvation in Ireland was the product of a natural disaster or of free-market economic policies (or both) is clearly beyond the remit of this column. On the specific issue of Vicky's charitableness, readers are as ever invited to correct errors or add new information, via the letters page.

SOURCES

http://multitext.ucc.ie/d/Private_Responses_to_the_Famine3344361812
www.bbc.co.uk/history/british/victorians/famine_01.shtml
www.battersea.org.uk/about_us/our_history